DEEP GLIMPSES

AUTHOR OF AUTHORITY

Authority Is Transferred through Worship

P.J. ALLAN

Published by Deep Glimpses
www.deepglimpses.com

Print ISBN: 979-8-9928260-4-3
E-book ISBN: 979-8-9928260-5-0

Printed in the United States

CONTENTS

INTRODUCTION: ASTONISHED BY AUTHORITY

The teachings of Jesus were remarkable to His audience, not only for their content but also for the authority with which He spoke (Matthew 7:28–29). This book examines the concept of genuine authority—how it is received rather than seized, and how it is expressed through respectful submission to God. For believers, the responsibility to communicate as representatives of God (1 Peter 4:11) necessitates alignment with the Holy Spirit instead of dependence on personal effort. This booklet aims to provide an in-depth analysis of the authority exemplified by Christ and its practical application for contemporary faith practice.

Setting the Stage: Jesus' Teaching and the Power of Authority

And so it was, when Jesus had ended these sayings, that the people were <u>astonished at His teaching</u>, for

He taught them as <u>one having authority</u>, and not as the scribes.

—Matthew 7:28–29[*]

At the end of the Sermon on the Mount, we have an interesting commentary regarding Jesus and the way He taught: "for He taught them as one having authority, and not as the scribes." He taught them as one HAVING authority. Is authority a possession or a position? Also, it's worth noting the effect this had on those hearing someone teach with authority—the people were ASTONISHED. When was the last time you were astonished after hearing someone teach? Should we expect those who proclaim the gospel to speak as those "having authority"?

The Call to Speak as Oracles of God

According to Peter, we should . . .

If anyone speaks, let him speak as the <u>oracles of God</u>. If anyone ministers, let him do it as with the ability which <u>God supplies</u>, that in all things God may be glorified through Jesus Christ, to whom <u>belong the glory and the dominion</u> forever and ever. Amen.

—1 Peter 4:11[*]

---

[*] Emphasis added

There is continuity between what Peter writes here and someone teaching with authority. I believe the key is that God, through Jesus Christ, is still allowed to have prominent occupancy of the message. In other words, we are teaching under the prompting of the Spirit of God, and the Spirit of God is the One teaching through us. He is in between the letters and the phrases. He saturates the words with comfort, edification, and conviction. We are not as Paul describes those who "beat the air," but we are in submission and partnership to the message coming from God Himself.

> *Do you not know that those who run in a race all run, but one receives the prize? Run in such a way that you may* <u>*obtain it*</u>*. And everyone who competes for the prize is temperate in all things. Now they do it to obtain a perishable crown, but we for an imperishable crown. Therefore I run thus: not with uncertainty. Thus I fight: not as one who* <u>*beats the air*</u>*. But I discipline my body and bring it into* <u>*subjection*</u>*, lest, when I have preached to others, I myself should become* <u>*disqualified*</u>*.*

> *—1 Corinthians 9:24-27*[*]

Paul here mentions a posture or qualifier that equips him with a foundation to be effective in his ministry. It is not just getting up there to speak and letting it rip. It is making sure you are in subjection or submission to the lordship of Christ

---

[*] Emphasis added

and that you are speaking under the unction of the Holy Spirit. Oh, if only more were this careful in their speech. There seems to be an accepted presumption these days that just because we are preaching the Word from the Bible, God is partnering with us automatically.

The Word of God does have intrinsic power in and of itself, but that does not release us from the obligation to be under the control of the Holy Spirit while we are proclaiming it. The scribes and pharisees taught from the Word—they taught the Law—but lacked life-changing power. Their words and message did not resonate with authority. Some can possess an authority in the Word that is acquired by certifications and degrees. That is a type of authority, and they can shout it out with the authority that comes from learning, yet lack the accompanying power of the Holy Spirit that gives the Word life and authentic power.

> *If the ax is dull, And one does not sharpen the edge, Then he must use more strength; But wisdom brings success.*
>
> *—Ecclesiastes 10:10*

The sharpening begins with a study of the Scripture, but it is honed to surgical precision by one who submits to the Holy Spirit so that the Word could, in fact, cut between joint and marrow, thoughts and intents of the heart.

> *So he answered and said to me:*
> *"This is the word of the LORD to Zerubbabel:*

Not by might nor by power, <u>but by My Spirit,</u>'
<u>*Says the LORD of hosts.*</u>
—Zechariah 4:6[*]

For the word of God is living and powerful, and sharper
than any two-edged sword, piercing even to the divi-
sion of soul and spirit, and of joints and marrow, and
is a discerner of the thoughts and intents of the heart.

—Hebrews 4:12

Let me be honest, I have been a preacher and teacher for over thirty-three years. (The difference between preach and teach is that preach has REACH in it.) I know the difference between proclaiming the Word in my own strength and heralding a message birthed in my heart by the Holy Spirit. Thankfully, God will use both, but when the Holy Spirit leads it, there is more of a transformation in the heart of the listener and not just an exchange of information.

Another factor contributing to a diminishment of authority while preaching a message is the teaching schedule imposed upon the pulpit ministry. This, in my opinion, is an over-taxing expectation and a system that places an amplified pressure on having to pump out messages. This forces the minister to go beyond their authentic, organic, and simple walk in obeying the Spirit to have a multitasking teaching of sermons or lectures in venues throughout the week. No wonder many

---

[*] Emphasis added

preachers lean heavily on and depend on academic periodical subscriptions or online sermon services for their messages rather than a message having authority from the Lord. Many just repeat what they were taught in seminary or Bible college, and they recirculate the same messages. Some may say they have had thirty years' experience in preaching, when in reality, they had one year of experience repeated thirty times.

In biblical times, you see how the disciples went from city to city preaching the gospel so that their audience or listeners changed regularly. Today, we gather the same people so that the messages need to change. What is God saying to us today? Now? Believe me, it is easier said than done.

CHAPTER 1: DEFINING AUTHORITY— POSSESSION OR POSITION?

L et us get back to asking whether having authority is a possession or a position. I was in the same position at the pulpit in both the above examples, but there was a difference when authority was in my possession and I knew it. The fact that many people have a position of authority, but not a true possession of authority, is the reason there is so much confusion about what real authority looks and sounds like. In my experience, it was the cause for me not to trust those in authority during the early part of my life. I saw it abused, misrepresented, or misunderstood. There is something un-settling when you experience someone who is supposed to be in a position of authority, but does not represent it well or in the right spirit. They lord over you, diminish you, or worse, manipulate, abuse, and try to control you.

Contrasting True Authority with Human Presumption: Lessons from the Sons of Sceva

A good example of someone presuming to operate without actual authority is the story of the sons of Sceva.

> *Now God worked unusual miracles by the hands of Paul, so that even handkerchiefs or aprons were brought from his body to the sick, and the diseases left them and the evil spirits went out of them. Then some of the itinerant Jewish exorcists <u>took it upon themselves</u> to call the name of the Lord Jesus over those who had evil spirits, saying, "We exorcise you by the Jesus whom Paul preaches." Also there were seven sons of Sceva, a Jewish chief priest, who did so.*
>
> *And the evil spirit answered and said, "Jesus I know, and Paul I know; but who are you?"*
>
> *Then the man in whom the evil spirit was leaped on them, overpowered them, and prevailed against them, so that they fled out of that house naked and wounded. This became known both to all Jews and Greeks dwelling in Ephesus; and <u>fear fell on them all</u>, and the name of the Lord Jesus was magnified.*
>
> *—Acts 19:11–17*[*]

What a dynamic contrast in comparing the cause and effect between Paul's effortless effectiveness and the sons of

---

[*] Emphasis added

Sceva. The static handkerchiefs or aprons brought from Paul's body had more power than the intrusive dynamic actions of the others. This is a dramatic and amplified example of someone taking upon themselves the right to cast out demons without the God-given authority to do so. The consequence of this overextension and presumptuous positioning is seen by them fleeing the house naked and wounded. But the bigger result was that fear fell on them all. This just got real. This was not a game.

The fear of the Lord is one of the components missing from self-entitled proclaimers, especially among those attempting spiritual warfare. The spirit world is real. They are not afraid to speak out in the place of God. Think about what we are called to do! What a formidable, frightening assignment.

> *For we do not wrestle against flesh and blood, but against principalities, against powers, against the rulers of the darkness of this age, against spiritual hosts of wickedness in the heavenly places.*
> *—Ephesians 6:12*

Missteps in Authority: The Sons of Thunder and Self-Appointed Power

Another illustration, a little closer to home, can be the example of James and John, the sons of Zebedee (sons of thunder), wanting to call down fire from heaven.

And when His disciples James and John saw this, they said, "Lord, do You want <u>us to command</u> fire to come down from heaven and consume them, just as Elijah did?" But He turned and <u>rebuked them,</u> and said, "You do not know <u>what manner of spirit you are of.</u> For the Son of Man did not come to destroy men's lives but to save them." And they went to another village.

—Luke 9:54–56[*]

They were trying to do something they thought was good and right in their own eyes, but it was in the wrong spirit. An interesting follow-up to this rebuke is another time when James and John's mother tried to get her sons into a higher authoritative position with Jesus.

Then the mother of Zebedee's sons came to Him with her sons, kneeling down and asking something from Him. And He said to her, "What do you wish?"

She said to Him, "Grant that these two sons of mine may sit, one on Your right hand and the other on the left, in Your kingdom."

But Jesus answered and said, "You do not know what you ask. Are you able to drink the cup that I am about to drink, and be baptized with the baptism that I am baptized with?"

They said to Him, "We are able."

---

[*] Emphasis added

So He said to them, "You will indeed drink My cup, and be baptized with the baptism that I am baptized with; but to sit on My right hand and on My left is not Mine to give, but it is for those for whom it is <u>prepared by My Father</u>."

And when the ten heard it, they were greatly displeased with the two brothers. But Jesus called them to Himself and said, "You know that the rulers of the Gentiles lord it over them, and those who are great exercise <u>authority over</u> them. <u>Yet it shall not be so among you; but whoever desires to become great among you, let him be your servant. And whoever desires to be first among you, let him be your slave—just as the Son of Man did not come to be served, but to serve, and to give His life a ransom for many</u>."

—Matthew 20:20–28[*]

We cannot put ourselves in a position of authority unless it is given to us by God. If God gives you a place in His body, it is the place you belong, and it cannot be taken away. There is a silent confidence without arrogance.

God is working in them, and
He makes them look good.

[*] Emphasis added

We look at leaders and can envy their position and assume we can do that as well. One of the problems with someone God has put in a position or possession of authority is that they can make it look easy. God is working in them, and He makes them look good. Some believe that Paul was not even aware that these items were taken from him.

Even handkerchiefs or aprons were brought from his body to the sick, and the diseases left them and the evil spirits went out of them.

It doesn't say that Paul sent these items, but rather they were brought from his body, which can imply people may have just taken these items off of Paul. If this is the case, we can see the beginnings of those who "take" authority.

CHAPTER 2: TAKING AUTHORITY

"Assuredly, I say to you, among those born of women there has not risen one greater than John the Baptist; but he who is least in the kingdom of heaven is greater than he. And from the days of John the Baptist until now the kingdom of heaven <u>suffers violence,</u> and the <u>violent take it by force.</u>

—Matthew 11:11–12[*]

After John the Baptist was arrested, before he was later beheaded, Jesus spoke about him to the crowd. He strongly endorsed John as a prophet foretold in the Scripture and compared him with previous prophets throughout history. When Jesus said that the "least in the kingdom is greater than he," it was because John was the last of the old covenant prophets. So anyone born again in the

_____

[*] Emphasis added

New Testament established by the blood of Jesus is "greater than he."

I do not believe the lesson Jesus was endorsing here is that anyone can "TAKE" the kingdom by force or violence. I believe He was referring to those who imprisoned John and ultimately executed him. If I remember correctly, that is exactly what Satan attempted to do with the throne of God.

Authority is something
you receive, not take!

The Illusion of Control: Why Authority Cannot Be Seized

Try taking authority in other areas of your life. If you see someone crashing a stop sign, chase them down and fine them—just take authority. Or while grocery shopping, if you see an unruly child, just take authority and discipline the child. So, how is that working for you? There is a God-given authority that can only be received and not taken. In fact, after His resurrection, Jesus breathed on His disciples and exhorted them to "receive" the Holy Spirit.

> So Jesus said to them again, "Peace to you! As the Father has sent Me, I also send you." And when He

had said this, He breathed on them, and said to them,
"Receive the Holy Spirit."

—John 20:21-22*

This was not their baptism, but rather Christ's admonishment to position themselves for what was about to be poured out upon them at Pentecost. Let us read the account in the first chapter of Acts.

And being assembled together with them, He commanded them not to depart from Jerusalem, but to wait for the Promise of the Father, "which," He said, "you have heard from Me; for John truly baptized with water, but you shall be baptized with the Holy Spirit not many days from now." Therefore, when they had come together, they asked Him, saying, "Lord, will You at this time restore the kingdom to Israel?" And He said to them, "It is not for you to know times or seasons which the Father has put in His own authority. But you shall receive power when the Holy Spirit has come upon you; and you shall be witnesses to Me in Jerusalem, and in all Judea and Samaria, and to the end of the earth."

—Acts 1:4-8*

---

* Emphasis added

Okay, in light of our subject, you have to look at verse 7, where Jesus told them of their limits in knowledge by saying: "It is not for you to know times or seasons which the Father has put in His own authority." Can you imagine the disciples saying, "Well, we're just going to TAKE AUTHORITY and demand this revelation from the Father?" I don't think so. Jesus said clearly, "IT IS NOT FOR YOU." But at the same time, He told them that they WOULD RECEIVE POWER to be His witnesses to the end of the earth.

Cultural Pitfalls: Entitlement and the Spirit of Envy

There is an entitlement among some teachers that would have you believe that we can just blab and grab. We can lay claim and pass blame. Blame is when it doesn't work. I believe this presumption of taking authority has crept into many teachers and leaders, which has led to dangerous and abusive validations of self-promotion and positional abuse. We might blame the American culture for emphasizing ambition and self-promotion as positive traits. We also battle a strong spirit of envy in our time. We think it is greed, but honestly, it is not that we are motivated to have more; it's that we just think we should be entitled to have what others have been given. Many with itching ears have supported these self-appointed and authority-taking teachers and have been motivated to take what these teachers present for their own gain as well.

Taking something has a completely different posture from receiving something. When I was pastoring a church, we never "took" an offering. It became clear in our culture that we would only "receive" offerings. Can you see the difference? Look around you and tell me what you see to be the difference in your own experiences. Taking has a demanding look of pride, of personal boldness and strength. *Receiving* has a humble posture, one who honors the giver and has thankfulness and praise toward the one they have received something from. "You will know them by their fruit" (Matt. 7:16). Now, can we be encouraged to "take" something that is being given to us by the Father? Yes, absolutely. If someone were handing you an extraordinary gift that you did not feel you deserved, and the giver of the gift said, "Take it," that is different from a person who just walks up to someone and grabs it out of their possession, forcefully or violently. That would be stealing. Have you ever given a gift to someone and afterward felt like the gift was taken and not received, with no appreciation or thankfulness; they just took it?

The Armor of God: Wearing Authority with Humility

I've seen the same presumption in referring to the SWORD found in Ephesians 6. I believe the desire to be clothed in the armor is appropriate, and we should pursue this covering. But we must first turn to God for this covering and receive Him as the one clothing us with His attributes. This is a lifelong attained covering. It is a transformational acquiring, not a simple conformity attire.

> And <u>take</u> the helmet of salvation, and the <u>sword of the Spirit</u>, which is the word of God.
>
> —Ephesians 6:17[*]

I looked up the word "take" in the Strong's Concordance (1209 in the Greek), and it is defined as "middle voice of a primary verb; <u>to receive</u> (in various applications, lit. or fig.); accept, receive, take." I could not count the number of messages I've heard from this text. Yet often, there are specific key aspects ignored or overlooked concerning the armor of God. Let me point out a few and see if you have noticed their absence as well. Let us start with, "be strong in the Lord and in the power of His might." This armor is not something we can wear in our own strength, no more than David could wear Saul's armor. It is not something we can put on and pound our chests as if we are now invincible. Every aspect of this varied provision is only found in the Lord Himself. There must be a humble dependency on His power and might for any of this to work effectively. The "whole armor of God" should be pretty clear and self-explanatory. The armor is His covering and His attributes that we receive from Him. Remember, Paul is using a metaphor of armor to explain a spiritual reality more focused on the outcome than the process. Most commentators believe Paul was referring to and comparing the Roman soldier's attire. I believe this makes a better example of what I am trying to say here. The soldier didn't own the uniform; it did not belong to him. The attire belonged to Rome. Only when he was in

---

[*] Emphasis added

the service of Rome and under the command of Rome did he have the authority to be fully vested with wielding his duties. Unless, of course, the soldier went rogue and started operating presumptuously and independently from command. It is the armor of God, and as such, we, too, must be submissive to His commands and directions.

There is much more I could develop here, but let me encapsulate what I've heard that bothered me the most and see if you agree. I have heard many say, "Take your sword, the Word of God, and use it against the enemy." Now my primary objection is that it's not YOUR sword to take. Beating someone with the knowledge you have gathered from Scripture is not the accurate and precise intention of the Holy Spirit. Keep it in His hands to be wielded for His purposes because, after all, it is the sword of the Spirit. This is why many use the sword of the Spirit as if it were a switchblade or a battle-axe in the hands of a street thug. Instead, it should be accurately cut like a surgeon with a scalpel. If we look at Hebrews 4:12 again, we can see its precise intended purpose.

> For the word of God is living and powerful, and sharper than any two-edged sword, piercing even to the division of soul and spirit, and of joints and marrow, and is a discerner of the thoughts and intents of the heart. And there is no creature hidden from His sight, but all things are naked and open to the eyes of Him to whom we must give account.
>
> —Hebrews 4:12–13

Precision in Power: The Sword of
the Spirit as a Surgical Tool

If you consider the specific application of the cuts made by the sword of His Word, you will see they are minuscule and precise cuts dividing between soul and spirit, between joints and marrow, and able to distinguish thoughts and intents of the heart . . . these are surgical cuts. You do not have to cut off the head to remove a blemish.

Hopefully, as we continue to discover the author of authority, this distinction will become clearer. So let us look at how this whole thing initially opened up to me.

CHAPTER 3: PERSONAL REALIZATION— OVERCOMING RESISTANCE TO AUTHORITY

But you do not believe, because you are not of My sheep, as I said to you. <u>My sheep hear My voice</u>, and I know them, and they follow Me."

—John 10:26–27[*]

As I mentioned earlier, my early years were marked by rebellion. I grew up in a home filled with constant fighting and alcohol abuse every day. My dad, an ex-marine with a drinking problem, asserted his authority through constant

---

[*] Emphasis added

put-downs, humiliations, and challenges to fight him. Physical and verbal abuse were the norm. Additionally, I lived in the inner city, where some officials in positions of authority were corrupt and exploited their office for personal gain. While there were many good examples, my perspective was skewed. Consequently, I developed a strong opposition to any form of authority.

God was not a strong part of my upbringing. I was raised by going to church every Sunday, but even there, I saw the leaders of the congregation living contrary lifestyles to their positions. This disillusionment led me into a life of drug abuse and violence. By the time I was nineteen, I was hanging around a motorcycle gang and abusing my life and health with full intensity . . . until I was radically saved on my twentieth birthday. I became totally consumed with involvement in the church to the extent that within a few years, I became a youth pastor and then, many years later, planted a church. But God was working deeper and deeper things in my heart. One of my struggles as a pastor was when I realized I was now in a position of authority, and I hated authority. Can anyone say *inner conflict*? I did not want to be called pastor. I shied away from being esteemed and hesitated to speak boldly into people's lives, until one day the Lord confronted me. I saw that I was not truly operating in the office God placed me in, and there needed to be a change in me. While in prayer about this issue, the Lord opened my understanding. I'm not sure how you stand with this or whether you can accept it, but the Lord spoke to me as I have heard Him speak often in my life. It was not an audible voice, but rather an instant communication with my thoughts. It was hearing a perspective that was outside and beyond my own understanding. All of a sudden, within a millisecond, I understood what was being said. So, allow me to extend that condensed and intensely intuitive exchange with a more conversational template. Okay? Here we go.

A Journey of Rebellion: From Resistance to Redemption

So, the Lord said: "I will give you three different words and you tell me how they make you feel." The first word was creativity. I love creativity. I am a musician and have written many songs, so creativity is a big part of my expression in life. God has given me a great imagination, so I enjoy coming up with flow charts, building projects, and organizational challenges. The second word was originality, which is also a word I applaud as a valid, unique expression of individuality and an important aspect of our identity. When you comprehend your own identity and realize there is no one else exactly like you, and you embrace that distinction, it is liberating and amazing. You are a completely unique individual made by God. You are the original you! I love creativity and originality. Then He said the word authority, and I literally felt like a wet, heavy blanket fell over me. It felt oppressive, controlling, restricting, and limiting. It quenched all the excitement I had over the previous two words. He went on to show me something else after that. He said to look at the first part of each word.

Creativity - Create
Originality - Origin
Authority - Author

These words are not contradictory or conflicting, but rather construct continuity. True authority has the power to create and originate. To create and originate makes you the authority of that which was made. So here I am, the author of this book—ha, go figure. The reason Jesus spoke with authority was because He is the Author, Creator, and Originator of all things.

Another parable He put forth to them, saying: "The kingdom of heaven is like a mustard seed, which a man took and sowed in his field, which indeed is the least of all the seeds; but when it is grown it is greater than the herbs and becomes a tree, so that the birds of the air come and nest in its branches."

> *Another parable He spoke to them: "The kingdom of heaven is like leaven, which a woman took and hid in three measures of meal till it was all leavened."*
>
> *All these things Jesus spoke to the multitude in parables; and without a parable He did not speak to them, that it might be fulfilled which was spoken by the prophet, saying: "I will open My mouth in parables;*
>
> *I will utter things kept secret from the foundation of the world."*
>
> *—Matthew 13:31-35*

Jesus spoke about seeds and leaven because He understood their processes from the beginning of creation. He spoke them into being, and this gave Him the authority over them.

> *He is the image of the invisible God, the firstborn over all creation. For by Him all things were created that are in heaven and that are on earth, visible and invisible, whether thrones or dominions or principalities or powers. All things were created through Him and for Him. And He is before all things, and in Him all things consist. And He is the head of the body, the church, who is the beginning, the firstborn from the dead, that in all things He may have the preeminence. For it pleased the Father that in Him all the fullness should dwell, and by Him to reconcile all things to Himself, by Him, whether things on earth or things in heaven, having made peace through the blood of His cross.*
>
> *—Colossians 1:15–20*

So, to answer my question, is authority a position or a possession? The real answer is both, but in the right order. The possession of authority is the essence that manifests, confirms, and establishes the position.

> *A man's gift makes room for him, And brings him before great men.*
>
> *—Proverbs 18:16*

Many believe the above verse is talking about a bribe. I guess that would make sense in the natural, but it also applies to the spiritual. If God has given you a gift, through transformational growth in grace, it will manifest in such a way that it will become evident to others, thereby making room. Jesus' authority was in His possession; Jesus had no certification as far as the Jews were concerned. He was the son of Mary and Joseph, the carpenter.

> Then they came again to Jerusalem. And as He was walking in the temple, the chief priests, the scribes, and the elders came to Him. And they said to Him, "By what authority are You doing these things? And who gave You this authority to do these things?"
>
> But Jesus answered and said to them, "I also will ask you one question; then answer Me, and I will tell you by what authority I do these things: The baptism of John—was it from heaven or from men? Answer Me."
>
> And they reasoned among themselves, saying, "If we say, 'From heaven,' He will say, 'Why then did you not believe him?' But if we say, 'From men'"—they feared the people, for all counted John to have been a prophet indeed. So they answered and said to Jesus, "We do not know."
>
> And Jesus answered and said to them, "Neither will I tell you by what authority I do these things."
>
> —Mark 11:27–33

It is interesting that even the leaders of His day recognized that authority was given. Jesus, knowing their hearts, gave them a similar question about John. This trapped them in a dilemma that either way they answered would expose their error in persecuting John. A couple of things to take away from this example:

- Authority is an important aspect in establishing you and your ministry.
- True authority is not always "certifiable" but is seen in its power.

I'm sorry to appear snarky in saying it this way, but it can be summarized: "You either have it, or you don't; you either know the Author, or you don't." Jesus intentionally set a snare in His rebuttal question, knowing they were unable to answer it correctly. Many times, Jesus referred to the works He did as His validation and credentials.

> *Jesus answered them, "I told you, and you do not be-lieve. The works that I do in My Father's name, they bear witness of Me. But you do not believe, because you are not of My sheep, as I said to you. My sheep hear My voice, and I know them, and they follow Me.*

> —John 10:25–27

His authority was a possession that came from an in-ternal position with God and made room for Him by His works. Likewise, someone who has studied hard and is truly knowledgeable concerning a specific subject may be considered an authority in that particular subject. They can tell you how it all began and how it works. They know its history and current state of operations. But there should be separate considerations and distinctions. Their authority came from knowledge and is established by knowledge, but not necessarily by God. So, give credit where credit is due. Respect and appreciate their academic learning and achievement.

> At times in our church history, we have made a slight turn from making disciples to making students instead.

I think this is part of the problem. Sometime in our church history, we made a slight turn from making disciples to making students instead. Someone becomes a Christian, and instead of emphasizing a slow and honest walk with God through prayer and the Word, we send them into a ten-week foundations course. The information in that class may be valid and indeed foundational for their growth, but did we just make a subtle shift, a mild nudge for them to pursue academics? I know that in 2 Timothy 2:15, the KJV says "study." But many versions have restated that.

> *Remind them of these things, charging them before the Lord not to strive about words to no profit, to the ruin of the hearers. Be diligent to present yourself*

> *approved to God, a worker who does not need to be ashamed, rightly dividing the word of truth. But shun profane and idle babblings, for they will increase to more ungodliness.*
>
> —*2 Timothy 2:14-17**

Academia is not what the world needs from the Church, but rather seeing the demonstration of the Spirit given to us in "love, power, and a sound mind." A sound mind, yes, but not one puffed up.

> *For God has not given us a spirit of fear, but of power and of love and of a sound mind.*
>
> —*2 Timothy 1:7*

> *Now these things, brethren, I have figuratively transferred to myself and Apollos for your sakes, that you may learn in us not to think beyond what is written, that none of you may be puffed up on behalf of one against the other. For who makes you differ from another? And what do you have that you did not receive? Now if you did indeed receive it, why do you boast as if you had not received it?*
>
> —*1 Corinthians 4:6-7*

---

* Emphasis added

We are going to discuss how we "receive" authority a little later.

> *Now some are puffed up, as though I were not coming to you. But I will come to you shortly, if the Lord wills, and I will know, not the word of those who are puffed up, but the power. For the kingdom of God is not in word <u>but in power</u>.*
>
> —*1 Corinthians 4:18–20**

> *Knowledge puffs up, but love edifies (builds up). And if anyone thinks that he knows anything, he knows nothing yet as he ought to know. <u>But if anyone loves God</u>, this one is <u>known by Him</u>.*
>
> —*1 Corinthians 8:1-3**

> *Grace and peace be multiplied to you in the <u>knowledge of God</u> and of Jesus our Lord, as His <u>divine power</u> has given to us all things that pertain <u>to life and godliness</u>, through the <u>knowledge of Him</u> who called us by glory and virtue, by which have been given to us exceedingly great and precious promises, that through these you may be partakers of the <u>divine nature</u>, having escaped the corruption that is in the world through lust. But also for this very reason, giving all diligence, <u>add*

---

* Emphasis added

to your faith virtue, to virtue knowledge, to knowledge self-control, to self-control perseverance, to perseverance godliness, to godliness brotherly kindness, and to brotherly kindness love. For if these things are yours and abound, you will be neither barren nor unfruitful in the knowledge of our Lord Jesus Christ. For he who lacks these things is shortsighted, even to blindness, and has forgotten that he was cleansed from his old sins.

Therefore, brethren, be even more diligent to make your call and election sure, for if you do these things you will never stumble; for so an entrance will be supplied to you abundantly into the everlasting kingdom of our Lord and Savior Jesus Christ.

—2 Peter 1:2–11[*]

Peter here speaks clearly that the knowledge we seek is to know God. It is true we get to know God through His Word, but Peter also states a sequence in verse 5, "Add to your faith *virtue, to virtue knowledge.*" The first step for a newfound faith is meant to be a pursuit of "virtue," then knowledge. When I looked up this word in *Strong's Concordance*, I have to admit I was quite surprised. I thought virtue meant "goodness," and yes, that is a part of it. But here is the definition: "manliness, (valor) excellence (intrinsic or attributed)—praise, virtue." So

---

[*] Emphasis added

31

our first lesson in newfound faith is "become a good man of valor."

This commission exposes the problem with positional authority. It is the difference between a good man and an educated man. The knowledge acquired can both serve as a blessing or a curse . . . one could become a smart crook. It is like someone who studies constitutional law for the purpose of destroying the constitution. It is like a gun that can be used for good or evil. It all depends on whose hand holds the gun.

I remember as a young believer, I attended a revival where the guest evangelist played guitar with Elvis Presley in his BC days (Before Christ). My past was rock 'n' roll music, so when I gave my life to Christ, I repented of the music I played. I put down my guitar and said, "I will not play it again." Well, this evangelist was killin' it with his guitar, if you like rockabilly. So after the meeting, I approached him and asked how he could play like that, being a Christian. I'll never forget his answer; he said, "The only thing that makes a guitar evil is an evil man playing it." Thank you, thank you very much.

With God, it is always an issue of the heart. When people get an education and gain knowledge without a good heart, they can be elevated in positions of authority and corrupt in their actions. I am sorry to say, but I have heard of many families who have sacrificed much in order to be able to send their kids through college, only to have them emerge an un-recognizable and somewhat twisted version of their past self, all because of so-called "higher learning." I used to say face-tiously, "God doesn't want us smarter, He wants us gooder."

Years ago, I gave a message from Proverbs 31:10–31, a passage that beautifully manifests the actions of virtue in real time. Unfortunately, in its context, it is primarily applied to a woman, which is a good thing. When I say unfortunately, it is because I believe men need to look at this as well. The word "virtue" is the feminine application, but it also has a masculine nuance. So you can interchange virtue and valor, in that the attribute can be applied to depict a feminine or masculine expression based on context. As women bear the brunt of the expectation of Proverbs 31, it would not hurt for a man to use this same text and evaluate, with slight varied applications, what a man of valor may look like . . . look at the attributes and the work ethic.

Herein lies the key to authority. It is based on a sequential and subordinate relationship to God established in the very beginning of creation itself. Let's take a look at some of the highlights of how this all began.

CHAPTER 4: THE BEGINNING OF AUTHORITY—GOD AS AUTHOR

In the beginning God created the heavens and the earth.

The law of "first mentions" notes that to understand a particular word or doctrine, we must find the first place in Scripture that word or doctrine is revealed and study that passage. The reasoning is that the Bible's first mention of a concept is the simplest and clearest presentation. Seeing we have learned that the word *author* is the basis for *authority*, 'In the beginning God' is the basis for everything that exists—He is Creator, Originator, and Author of everything seen and unseen.

> *The earth was without form, and void; and darkness was on the face of the deep. And the Spirit of God was*

hovering over the face of the waters. Then God said, "Let there be light"; and there was light. And God saw the light, that it was good; and God divided the light from the darkness. God called the light Day, and the darkness He called Night. So the evening and the morning were the first day.

—Genesis 1:1-5

Then God said, "Let Us make man in Our image, according to Our likeness; let them have dominion over the fish of the sea, over the birds of the air, and over the cattle, over all the earth and over every creeping thing that creeps on the earth." So God created man in His own image; in the image of God He created him; male and female He created them. Then God blessed them, and God said to them, "Be fruitful and multiply; fill the earth and subdue it; have dominion over the fish of the sea, over the birds of the air, and over every living thing that moves on the earth."

—Genesis 1:26–28

Then the LORD God took the man and put him in the Garden of Eden to tend and keep it. And the LORD God commanded the man, saying, "Of every tree of the garden you may freely eat; but of the tree of the knowledge of good and evil you shall not eat, for in the day that you eat of it you shall surely die."

—Genesis 2:15–17

Out of the ground the LORD God formed every beast of the field and every bird of the air, and brought them to Adam to see what he would call them. And whatever Adam called each living creature, that was its name. So Adam gave names to all cattle, to the birds of the air, and to every beast of the field.

—Genesis 2:19–20*

The Fall and Loss of Authority: Man's Disobedience

Now the serpent was more cunning than any beast of the field which the LORD God had made. And he said to the woman, "Has God indeed said, 'You shall not eat of every tree of the garden'?"

And the woman said to the serpent, "We may eat the fruit of the trees of the garden; but of the fruit of the tree which is in the midst of the garden, God has said, 'You shall not eat it, nor shall you touch it, lest you die.'"

Then the serpent said to the woman, "You will not surely die. For God knows that in the day you eat of it your eyes will be opened, and you will be like God, knowing good and evil."

---

* Emphasis added

So when the woman saw that the tree was good for food, that it was pleasant to the eyes, and a tree desirable to make one wise, she took of its fruit and ate. She also gave to her husband with her, and he ate. Then the eyes of both of them were opened, and they knew that they were naked; and they sewed fig leaves together and made themselves coverings.

—Genesis 3:1–7

So the LORD God said to the serpent: "Because you have done this, You are cursed more than all cattle, And more than every beast of the field; On your belly you shall go, And you shall eat dust All the days of your life. And I will put enmity Between you and the woman, And between your seed and her Seed; <u>He shall bruise your head, And you shall bruise His heel.</u>"

—Genesis 3:14–15**

Okay, I know that was a lot to take in, but allow me to give you the highlights.

God created the universe and everything in it, making Him the Author of all things.

God created man and woman and gave them dominion (delegated authority, under Him) over the earth to tend and keep it. The fact that God allowed man to name all the animals

---

* Emphasis added

demonstrates the authority given to man. He spoke creatively and originally.

God set up a limitation and instruction for man to follow. He gave him access to everything in the Garden except for one tree and forbade him from eating of its fruit. Once again, as I referred to earlier concerning the disciples questioning Jesus and wanting to know about the end times in Acts chapter 1, Jesus answered them by saying, "It's NOT for you to know."

The serpent (the adversary of God) tempted them with the one thing they couldn't have, which is a scheme he still uses and has not changed to this day. The adversary will always make you look at your lack instead of all that you've already been given. The problem arises when you are not looking at what you have but rather focusing on what you want that others have—envy!

They took the forbidden fruit. This made a radical change in the relational, sequential connection to God. Previously, God would come and fellowship with them in the cool of the day, and man had direct contact. So the sequential chain of relationship was God > Man > Creation. But after the violating act, the sequential order changed to God > Adversary > Man > Creation. Once man chose to believe the adversary, consequentially not believing God, he brought man under his control and power. Man forfeited his authority and dominion when he chose to submit to and believe the Adversary.

There was a prophetic promise made to the adversary by God: "And I will put enmity between you and the woman, And between your seed and her Seed; <u>He shall bruise your head, And you shall bruise His heel</u>" (emphasis added).

Now, let's cut to the heart of this issue. The reason Jesus was incarnate into flesh was so that He would restore man to his rightful place of authority under God by defeating the adversary and ransoming fallen mankind from the consequential bondage of sin. In the book of 1 Corinthians, Jesus is referred to as the last Adam.

> *And so it is written, "The first man Adam became a living being." The last Adam became a life-giving spirit. However, the spiritual is not first, but the natural, and afterward the spiritual. The first man was of the earth, made of dust; the second Man is the Lord from heaven. As was the man of dust, so also are those who are made of dust; and as is the heavenly Man, so also are those who are heavenly. And as we have borne the image of the man of dust, we shall also bear the image of the heavenly Man.*
>
> *—1 Corinthians 15:45–49*

CHAPTER 5: THE SHOWDOWN— AUTHORITY CHALLENGED AND RECLAIMED

Then Jesus, being filled with the Holy Spirit, returned from the Jordan and was <u>led by the Spirit</u> into the wilderness, being tempted for forty days by the devil. And in those days He ate nothing, and afterward, when they had ended, He was hungry.

And the devil said to Him, "If You are the Son of God, command this stone to become bread."

But Jesus answered him, saying, "It is written, Man shall not live by bread alone, but by every word of God."

> *Then the devil, taking Him up on a high mountain, showed Him all the kingdoms of the world in a moment of time. And the devil said to Him, "<u>All this authority I will give You, and their glory; for this has been delivered to me, and I give it to whomever I wish</u>.*
>
> *—Luke 4:1-6*[*]

(It would not surprise me if this encounter happened at high noon. ☺)

Here, the devil shows his trophy case of what "has been delivered" to him by man. I believe he knew that Jesus had come to get it back. He said that all this authority was given to him, and its glory, and he could give it to whomever he wished, again, proving that authority is, in fact, a substance that can be exchanged or imparted. Here is where he overplayed his hand and gave us tremendous insight into how this exchange transpires and how we can "receive" authority.

> *Therefore, if You will worship before me, all will be Yours."*
>
> *—Luke 4:7*

BA-BOOM!

---

[*] Emphasis added

The Key Revelation: Authority Is
Transferred through Worship

The devil was offering Jesus a shortcut to what He came to redeem. In essence, he was saying, "I know why you're here, and I know what you have come to do. I can give it to you ONLY if you keep me in the loop." So after this deal, the presumed sequential structure would be . . .

God > Adversary > Jesus > Man > Creation.

> *And Jesus answered and said to him, "Get <u>behind Me</u>, Satan! For it is written, You <u>shall worship</u> the LORD your God, and Him only you <u>shall serve</u>."'*
>
> —*Luke 4:8*

Jesus said, "NO DEAL." In fact, I'm here to go over your head, and when I do, you will bruise my heel, and I will bruise your head. Genesis prophecy fulfilled!

Remember Genesis 3:14–15 says, "So the LORD God said to the serpent: Because you have done this, You are cursed more than all cattle, And more than every beast of the field; On your belly you shall go, And you shall eat dust All the days of your life. And I will put enmity Between you and the woman, And between your seed and her Seed; <u>He shall bruise your head, And you shall bruise His heel</u>."*

---

* Emphasis added

CHAPTER 6:
TRANSFER OF
AUTHORITY
THROUGH WORSHIP

T here is another key that we could easily overlook here, and that is AUTHORITY IS TRANSFERRED THROUGH WORSHIP. This is HUGE. If we can get a handle on this, it would change everything. So the prerequisite to having authority is that you are first a true worshipper *under authority*. You are one under the lordship of Jesus Christ in real time. You worship and serve Him continuously. Your greatest joy is to be in His presence every day. You long for His presence, and only there are you content and fulfilled.

Have you ever wondered where this whole worship thing is going? The evolution of worship throughout church history is an interesting study. From Handel's Messiah, to converted bar tunes and changing them into church hymns, to contemporary Christian folk songs, to mega-ticket-selling concerts with laser beams and smoke machines. Is it just me, or has some of the contemporary worship industry subtly turned into the battle of the bands? I love music, especially really good music. I have binge-watched many worship videos, but after a while, it was hard to see or experience worship.

> ## True worship is putting yourself in the position of being under someone else's authority.

Real worship is not just music and singing songs. Music can be a way to accompany or escort you in worship, but true worship is putting yourself in the position of being under someone else's authority. By worshipping, you are giving the object of your worship the right to rule and reign over you. You are giving dominion over your decisions and choices, your possessions and wealth. Jesus said, as if interchangeable, the words "worship" and "serve." If you want to see who or what you worship, you can easily find out by looking at two things in your life—your checkbook and your calendar. It's where you give your strength, time, and resources.

Another expression for understanding what we mean when we say worship is WORTHSHIP. It is giving high esteem and priority to someone or something of irreplaceable value. Now, it can be a subtle shift from worshipping Jesus to worshipping worship. It could happen in other areas of our lives. We love LOVE, we love to sing about love, we love to fall in love, but oftentimes, we really don't love well. The heart of worship is to the Father, Son, and Holy Spirit—not the feeling we get or the excitement of a well-produced song.

Years ago, I saw a poster that was meant to demonstrate this subtle shift. At the time, Keith Green was a popular musician in Christian music. The picture was of a young person carrying a huge family Bible with a large wooden cross around his neck, saying, "I accepted Keith Green at a Jesus concert." Missed it by that much, but you get the point here. What if our worship was meant to be more? More than just an experience, but rather a meeting place of exchange, of empowerment, or even an endowment, that establishes a relational conduit for the impartation of authority.

I don't know why, but when I picture the essence of worship, I always see a medieval squire becoming a knight. You may have seen a movie or documentary of a knighting ceremony. They kneel before their king or queen. The sovereign would take a ceremonial sword and touch each shoulder, dubbing them into an elevated status of knighthood. It is all rather ceremonial, dignified, and eloquent when you see it done today. But when I think about it, I go back to the first king who thought this was an innovative idea. I do not know all the specifics of this historical event, but I do know there were always traitors and people trying to undermine the acquisition of power.

I imagine the trust factors within the court were under great suspicion, and it was important to prove one's loyalty and whether or not they could be brought into confidence. I did learn that one of the preferred ways to eliminate a rival was by poisoning, especially among those in competition within the same contemporary social circle. Everyone was well aware of how easily this could be accomplished. A customary practice was that before anyone drank together, they would pour their drink into each other's glasses to assure the other person that they did not poison the drink. If you trusted the person making this gesture, you would tap away their glass before they poured it, showing them that you did not think they would poison you. That's how toasting glasses came into being. We raise our glasses and tap each other's glasses, showing our friendship and trust.

So it was in this environment of suspicion that the king decided he would select men he could trust and bring them into his inner circle. I mean, this tradition had to start somewhere. So after proving a man's servitude as a squire, it was time for him to be brought into a new level of trust and authority. Picture the first time . . . the king would have the man kneel before him. He had to humble himself before the king and make himself vulnerable. While he was in that surrendered, defenseless position, the king took out his sword and put it at the man's throat. Imagine the intensity of that moment. The king, with a flick of his wrist, could have fatally wounded him. I see it as the potential knight giving his life into the king's hands. I could not find a record of the first time this knighting ceremony began, but I imagine there were words exchanged, maybe a vow. In essence, the exchange would establish that this man's life is now in the king's hands to do with as he wishes. Only after he totally surrendered his life could the king trust him with matters of the kingdom. Now, once knighted, he was *given a sword* of the kingdom, which enabled him to execute justice and judgment on behalf of the king . . . he was given authority *under* the king's command.

So again, *authority is transferred through worship.* Let's take a closer look at these attributes, attitudes, and posture that blend into a worship experience in spirit and truth.

Worship Starts with True Humility

The first aspect of a worshiper to consider is humility. I always look at the countenance of a worship leader—are they proud or humble? The oxymoron here in the corporate worship scenario is to put the worship leaders on a stage with a full amplified band, floodlights, and fog machines with screaming fans singing along with their favorite recorded songs and expecting them to be humble. I am not criticizing here; I pray for these leaders seriously and on a regular basis, and you should also. I can't even imagine the temptations they have to wrestle through just to keep their walk with Christ intact. To worship, one must put their own self in a subordinate position. If you are lifting someone or something above you in praise and adoration, you position yourself under them. Your focus in worship will be on what or who is most important to you. We have to realize that our worship extends way beyond the group worship experience and must be a daily priority. Not a "have to" but a strong, longing "want to" be with the one you worship.

> *Therefore <u>submit</u> to God. Resist the devil and he will flee from you. <u>Draw near</u> to God and He will draw near to you. Cleanse your hands, you sinners; and purify your hearts, you double-minded. Lament and mourn and weep! Let your laughter be turned to mourning and your joy to gloom. <u>Humble yourselves in the sight of the Lord, and He will lift you up.</u>*
>
> *—James 4:7–10[*]*

Everything in the above verses from James can be seen as aspects of worship. Submit to God, draw near to God, resist the devil, cleanse your hands, purify your hearts, lament, mourn, and weep. Humble yourself in His sight, and He will lift you

---

[*] Emphasis added

up. Previously, in reading this part on humbling ourselves, I envisioned myself kneeling before Him, humbling myself, and then He would lift me to stand before Him. But now that is not what I see at all. What I believe He is saying is that we should humble ourselves in His hand by kneeling, then He will lift us kneeling in His hand. His hand raises us up. Our position before Him never changes, no matter how high He lifts us up. We are always humble before the Lord and kneel in His hands. As we continue in our humility before Him, He will lift us up to heavenly places.

> *Let this mind be in you which was also in Christ Jesus, who, being in the form of God, did not consider it rob-bery to be equal with God, but made Himself of no reputation, taking the form of a bondservant, and coming in the likeness of men. And being found in*

appearance as a man, He <u>humbled Himself</u> and became obedient to the point of death, even the death of the cross. Therefore God also has highly exalted Him and given Him the name which is above every name, that at the name of Jesus <u>every knee should bow, of those in heaven, and of those on earth, and of those under the earth, and that every tongue should confess that Jesus Christ is Lord, to the glory of God the Father.</u>

—Philippians 2:5–11[*]

But God, who is rich in mercy, because of His great love with which He loved us, even when we were dead in trespasses, made us alive together with Christ (by grace you have been saved), and <u>raised us up together, and made us sit together in the heavenly places in Christ Jesus,</u> that in the ages to come He might show the exceeding riches of His grace in His kindness toward us in Christ Jesus. For by grace you have been saved through faith, and that not of yourselves; it is the gift of God, not of works, lest anyone should boast. For we are <u>His workmanship,</u> created in Christ Jesus for good works, which God prepared beforehand that we should walk in them.

—Ephesians 2:4–10

---

[*] Emphasis added

If we could truly comprehend the complete work of God's grace in our lives, we would stop striving for His acceptance and humbly receive all He has done—and is doing—to work His salvation in us to its glorious manifestation through our lives. He lifts us up, not based on our merit, but on His "prepared beforehand" works we are destined to complete.

The Centurion

Now when Jesus had entered Capernaum, a centurion came to Him, pleading with Him, saying, "Lord, my servant is lying at home paralyzed, dreadfully tormented." And Jesus said to him, "I will come and heal him."

The centurion answered and said, "Lord, I am not worthy that You should come under my roof. But only speak a word, and my servant will be healed. For I also am a man under authority, having soldiers under me. And I say to this one, 'Go,' and he goes; and to another, 'Come,' and he comes; and to my servant, 'Do this,' and he does it."

When Jesus heard it, He marveled, and said to those who followed, "Assuredly, I say to you, I have not found such great faith, not even in Israel! And I say to you that many will come from east and west, and sit down with Abraham, Isaac, and Jacob in the kingdom of heaven. But the sons of the kingdom will be cast out into outer darkness. There will be weeping and gnashing of teeth." Then Jesus said to the centurion, "Go your way; and as you have believed, so let it be done for you." And his servant was healed that same hour.

—Matthew 8:5–13[*]

Here was a man outside the people of promise in his day. He was actually a Roman centurion, a leader who had 100 men under his command—but only while he was under the command of Rome. Because of his unique position, he saw something in Jesus that others missed. Let's just say he was in middle management. He saw that Jesus was not an independent, solo operator, but that He was getting His orders from His commander or, in Christ's case, His Father. Jesus was first under authority, and that is why He had authority.

Jesus was first under authority, and that is why He had authority.

There's a different look on someone who is full of themselves, independent, or proud, with a savvy sway, but someone who is under authority has a softer, gentler, humbler approach. That is, unless he receives orders for forceful action, like clearing out the temple. There is only one Author of all things, so we can only receive authority from one source. Jesus came to

[*] Emphasis added

earth to show us the way to walk out this life on earth. Come under the Author of authority and live the life God created you to live. Jesus Himself bore witness to this fact in John.

> *Philip said to Him, "Lord, show us the Father, and it is sufficient for us."*
>
> *Jesus said to him, "Have I been with you so long, and yet you have not known Me, Philip? He who has seen Me has seen the Father; so how can you say, 'Show us the Father'? Do you not believe that I am in the Father, and the Father in Me? The words that I speak to you <u>I do not speak on My own authority</u>; but the Father who dwells in Me does the works. Believe Me that I am in the Father and the Father in Me, or else believe Me for the sake of the works themselves.*
>
> *—John 14:8-11**

Here again, in John 5, the Jewish leaders challenged His actions because He healed a man on the Sabbath.

> *For this reason the Jews persecuted Jesus, and sought to kill Him, because He had done these things on the Sabbath. But Jesus answered them, "My Father has been working until now, and I have been working." Therefore the Jews sought all the more to kill Him, because He not only broke the Sabbath, but also said that God was His Father, making Himself equal with*

---

* Emphasis added

God. Then Jesus answered and said to them, "Most assuredly, I say to you, <u>the Son can do nothing of Himself, but what He sees the Father do</u>; for whatever He does, the Son also does in like manner. For the Father loves the Son, and shows Him all things that He Himself does; and He will show Him greater works than these, that you may marvel. For as the Father raises the dead and gives life to them, even so the Son gives life to whom He will. For the Father judges no one, but has committed all judgment to the Son, that all should honor the Son just as they honor the Father. He who does not honor the Son does not honor the Father who sent Him.

"Most assuredly, I say to you, he who hears My word and believes in Him who sent Me has everlasting life, and shall not come into judgment, but has passed from death into life. Most assuredly, I say to you, the hour is coming, and now is, when the dead will hear the voice of the Son of God; and those who hear will live. For as the Father has life in Himself, so He has granted the Son to have life in Himself, and has given Him authority to execute judgment also, because He is the Son of Man. Do not marvel at this; for the hour is coming in which all who are in the graves will hear His voice and come forth—those who have done good, to the resurrection of life, and those who have done evil, to the resurrection of condemnation. I can of Myself do *nothing. As I hear, I judge; and My judgment is righteous, because I do not seek My own will but the will of the Father who sent Me.*

—*John 5:16–30*[*]

Another example of someone under authority, besides Jesus, is the archangel Michael in the book of Jude. The book of Jude deals strongly with those who have assumed positions of influence and authority. He points to some of the signs to recognize those who could be called "loose cannons." He also points to Old Testament examples.

> *Yet Michael the archangel, in contending with the devil, when he disputed about the body of Moses, dared not bring against him a reviling accusation, but said, "The Lord rebuke you!" (under authority) But these speak evil of whatever they do not know; and whatever they know naturally, like brute beasts, in these things they corrupt themselves. Woe to them! For they have gone in the way of Cain, have run greedily in the error of Balaam for profit, and perished in the rebellion of Korah.*

—*Jude 1:9–11*

Woe to them! Woe!

If you were to look at the following three Old Testament examples, you would see a common thread. Each of these

---

[*] Emphasis added

offenders "took authority" on themselves and for themselves. Cain took the authority to kill his brother. Balaam took authority to curse the people of God for money. And Numbers 16 tells how Korah took authority against Moses and gathered a group unto himself—this did not end well. This leads me to another concern; I've heard this often, and every time I do, the hair on the back of my neck stands up, and I fear for them. Woe! You may have heard it too? It's when these teachers shout boldly for you to "take authority," or in their own declaration of faith, they "take authority." I mean, I get it. They are stepping out over limitations that we can put on ourselves, limiting the power of God to move beyond our own doubts and fears. I get it, but that does not give you the right to just take it either. The archangel Michael did not take authority over the devil but was there by the will of God and said, "The Lord rebuke you." It is not faith that is executed when someone takes authority; it can be presumption, like in Saul's case with 1 Samuel.

> *As for Saul, he was still in Gilgal, and all the people followed him trembling. Then he waited seven days, according to the time set by Samuel. But Samuel did not come to Gilgal; and the people were scattered from him. So Saul said, "Bring a burnt offering and peace offerings here to me." And he offered the burnt offering. Now it happened, as soon as he had finished presenting the burnt offering, that Samuel came; and Saul went out to meet him, that he might greet him.*

> *And Samuel said, "What have you done?"*

Saul said, "When I saw that the people were scattered from me, and that you did not come within the days appointed, and that the Philistines gathered together at Michmash, then I said, 'The Philistines will now come down on me at Gilgal, and I have not made supplication to the LORD.' Therefore I felt compelled, and offered a burnt offering."

And Samuel said to Saul, "You have done foolishly. You have not kept the commandment of the LORD your God, which He commanded you. For now the LORD would have established your kingdom over Israel forever. But now your kingdom shall not continue. The LORD has sought for Himself a man after His own heart, and the LORD has commanded him to be commander over His people, because you have not kept what the LORD commanded you."

—1 Samuel 13:7-14

The other thing Jesus points out concerning the centurion in Matthew 8 was that his understanding of authority had affected his faith. It was of such significance that it caused Jesus to marvel. If we can really get a handle on what true authority is and how it operates, it will affect the level of our faith. We will be able to believe stronger, just as the centurion believed for his servant's healing, because we first know our place under authority. Then, when prompted by His Word or the Holy Spirit, we can move with an assurance that God is moving within us. And don't forget that according to Hebrews 12:2, Jesus is the Author and FINISHER of our faith.

> Looking unto Jesus, the <u>author and finisher</u> of our faith.

> —Hebrews 12:2[*]

What HE started in us HE will complete. Jesus is the "Author" of our faith, the Creator and Originator, which is why we must be under Him in order to represent Him. Like a kneeling knight, surrendering his life to serve and carry out the commands of his king, we, too, should be in the position of kneeling in worship, offering adoration and thankful praise to our King of Kings. In this continued posture of worship, we receive His authority, and our faith continues to grow. We can now operate under His lordship and influence the world around us with His Word spoken through us.

Jesus is the Author and FINISHER of our faith.

[*] Emphasis added

Worship Should Cost Us Something

Another aspect of worship is that worship should personally cost us something! There is something offered, something of worth, proving that we value who we worship more than any other thing in our lives.

> And Gad came that day to David and said to him, "Go up, erect an altar to the LORD on the threshing floor of Araunah the Jebusite." So David, according to the word of Gad, went up as the LORD commanded. Now Araunah looked, and saw the king and his servants coming toward him. So Araunah went out and bowed before the king with his face to the ground.
>
> Then Araunah said, "Why has my lord the king come to his servant?"
>
> And David said, "To buy the threshing floor from you, to build an altar to the LORD, that the plague may be withdrawn from the people."
>
> Now Araunah said to David, "Let my lord the king take and offer up whatever seems good to him. Look, here are oxen for burnt sacrifice, and threshing implements and the yokes of the oxen for wood. All these, O king, Araunah has given to the king."
>
> And Araunah said to the king, "May the LORD your God accept you."

Then the king said to Araunah, "No, but I will surely buy it from you for a price; <u>nor will I offer burnt offerings to the LORD my God with that which costs me nothing</u>." So David bought the threshing floor and the oxen for fifty shekels of silver. And David built there an altar to the LORD, and offered burnt offerings and peace offerings. So the LORD heeded the prayers for the land, and the plague was withdrawn from Israel.

—2 Samuel 24:18-25[*]

David understood a principle that there is a sacrifice involved in worship; there is a cost.

I beseech you therefore, brethren, by the mercies of God, that you present <u>your bodies a living sacrifice</u>, holy, acceptable to God, which is your <u>reasonable service</u> (true and proper worship NIV) And do not be <u>conformed</u> to this world, but be <u>transformed</u> by the renewing of your mind, that you may <u>prove</u> what is that good and acceptable and perfect will of God.

—Romans 12:1-2[*]

Paul writes to the Romans that they should present themselves as "living sacrifices." This is an oxymoron; it is like saying, "jumbo shrimp." They are opposites. But the problem with living sacrifices is that they keep crawling off the altar. Worship puts us back on the altar again and again, offering

---

[*] Emphasis added

our lives as living sacrifices (cost). There is something else here worth pondering. Let me ask you a question: Is your worship experience one of conformity or transformation? Usually, in a congregational setting, I would have to say it's conformity. We all sing the same songs at the same time because the worship leader is leading us together, with the same words on the screens. Even the cultural experience is conformity. Is it a wild, expressive culture, or is it a subdued and restrained culture? Either establishes both an expectation of our worship expression as well as limitations in order to fit in. Conformity is a quick response to just follow along. Transformation may be taking place, but it is a slower, gradual process, almost unnoticeable. It will eventually show itself in long-term consistency and enduring fruit, not just a temporary high.

Worship Is Transformational:
CONFORM OR TRANSFORM

> *Now the Lord is the Spirit; and where the Spirit of the Lord is, there is liberty. But we all, with unveiled face, beholding <u>as in a mirror</u> the glory of the Lord, are being <u>transformed</u> into the <u>same image</u> from glory to glory, just as by the Spirit of the Lord.*
>
> *—2 Corinthians 3:17–18*[*]

---

[*] Emphasis added

Here, we can see that this encounter with the Spirit is meant to be liberating and transformative. Let's look into something here . . . the mirror. Why a mirror? It could read "beholding as in a fire the glory of the Lord" or anything else, for that matter, so why a mirror? Beholding **as in a mirror** *the glory of the Lord.* This actually gives us huge insight into our psyche. We become what we worship.

I believe when we truly encounter the presence of the Lord in our worship, we see all His glorious attributes and characteristics: His love, patience, compassion, justice, holiness, glory, and the list is endless. In that same reflection of His glory, we can also see ourselves at the same time. We see Him seeing us, the real, authentic us. We see our need for Him; we see our shortcomings, weaknesses, and our brokenness, but He doesn't leave us in that state, nor does He condemn us. While we behold His glory, we are then being TRANSFORMED into His image from glory to glory. In some cases, it may feel more like gory to gory . . . it can get messy, but it's always for the good.

We become what we worship.

Speaking of messy, I cannot ignore what is happening in our secular culture. TRANS has become a big deal. People are becoming TRANS. I cannot help but think that this is a ploy of our enemy to take something valid, spiritual and life-changing, and pervert it, distort it, and commercialize it. At the same time, it is proving my point—you become what you worship!

Today, we have a deluge of "influencers" in sports and entertainment who are easily made into idols or icons. They can propagate lifestyles and life choices that highly influence young, developing hearts and minds. When ideals, delusions, and grandiose popular fads get hold of a generation, they worship it. The unfortunate outcome is when they discover they worshipped a delusion, a lie. My encouragement to them is to change what they worship.

Becoming What We Worship: The Mirror of God's Presence

We see ourselves through the eyes of who or what we worship. I compare this to a funhouse mirror. Have you ever seen yourself in one of these? One mirror is twisted in a way to make you look tall and slender (I prefer that mirror), while another mirror is twisted in a way that makes you look short and wide (I walk quickly past that one). When we worship God, we look into the only pure mirror that gives us our true reflection as seen through the eyes of someone who loves us unconditionally.

> *Therefore gird up the loins of your mind, be sober, and rest your hope fully upon the grace that is to be brought to you at the revelation of Jesus Christ; as*

obedient children, <u>not conforming yourselves</u> to the former lusts, as in your ignorance; but as He who called you is holy, you also be holy in all your conduct, because it is written, "Be holy, for I am holy."

—1 Peter 1:13–16[*]

All of Him, all of who He is, becomes available to us in worship, and in this mutually vulnerable transparency, everything He is has become accessible to us.

- His glory—we are transformed from glory to glory.
- His holiness—we are transformed from holy to holy.
- His authority—we are transformed from authority to authority.

Our level of submission, laying down our lives in obedience to His voice, determines what He can deposit in trust and authority. This is not a "works" thing; it's a "growth" thing. I believe God has already given us everything we need for this life and for godliness. But the question is, are we able to operate in and walk out that endowment with authentic authority?

As His divine power has given to <u>us all things that pertain to life and godliness</u>, through the knowledge of Him who called us by glory and virtue, by which have been given to us exceedingly great and precious promises, that through these you may be partakers of the divine nature, having escaped the corruption that is in the world through lust.
—2 Peter 1:3–4[*]

---

[*] Emphasis added

Non-conformity is not transformation; it's rebellion.

We are transformed into the image we behold in transformational worship. There is a world of difference between conforming and being transformed. So what's the difference between conformity and transformation? Conformity is compliance with an external pressure or expectation. It is fitting in, going with the flow. Driving the speed limit or using your fork when dining out are both small examples. We all conform to some extent just to get along in this world. A word of caution here: Non-conformity is not transformation; it's rebellion. But transformation is different; it starts from within you and then unfurls. This is what happens to a fruit tree when it is time to bear its fruit. Our worship could have some conformity, but it should be mostly transformation. If you've ever seen a decorated Christmas tree, it's a tree being conformed to customs and styles. On the other hand, the transformational manifestation of a live evergreen tree is pine cones. They came out from the inside, not the opposite. As believers, we can do the same thing. We hang good works or right behavior on ourselves in social platforms or inner circles. The Bible warns us of this practice:

> *Beware of false prophets, who come to you in sheep's clothing, but inwardly they are ravenous wolves. You will know them by their fruits.*
> *—Matthew 7:15–16**

---

* Emphasis added

It's easy for a wolf to look like a sheep. All he has to do is conform. Conformity is camouflage. Complying with external expectations will not produce internal fruit. Fruit, like a pine cone, comes from the inside out. The fruit of the wolf is ravenous and can only kill, steal, or destroy. Worship is meant to come from the inside out, not from the outside in. You will never bear fruit in conformity; fruitfulness can only happen through transformation.

Conformity is camouflage.

But the fruit of the Spirit is love, joy, peace, longsuffering, kindness, goodness, faithfulness, gentleness, self-control. Against such there is no law. And those who are Christ's have crucified the flesh with its passions and desires. If we live in the Spirit, let us also walk in the Spirit.

—Galatians 5:22–25

Our only hope of ever showing forth the authentic fruit of the Spirit is whether or not we emphasize a transformational walk over a conformity culture.

Therefore, my beloved, as you have always obeyed, not as in my presence only, but now much more in my absence, work out your own salvation with fear and trembling; for it is God who works in you both to will and to do for His good pleasure.

*—Philippians 2:12-13**

I think this is easier to understand if you look at verse 13 first, then verse 12. For God, working in you both to will and to do His good pleasure, so work out your own salvation with fear and trembling.

WORK OUT WHAT GOD IS WORKING IN.

I believe discerning the difference in whether or not your worship expression is one of conformity or transformation is an essential connection to whether you have true authority and you are bearing the fruit of the Spirit.

> *But know this, that in the last days perilous times will come: For men will be lovers of themselves, lovers of money, boasters, proud, blasphemers, disobedient to parents, unthankful, unholy, unloving, unforgiving, slanderers, without self-control, brutal, despisers of good, traitors, headstrong, haughty, lovers of pleasure rather than lovers of God, having a form of godliness but denying its power.*
>
> *—2 Timothy 3:1-5*

---

* Emphasis added

"Having a form of godliness but denying its power." Form is outside; power is inside. The power comes with transformation, and authentic growth comes from the inside out. Once you are in a culture of conformity, you've learned the acceptable guidelines, you know how to play the game, and so the outside behavior is now fashionable and fits into your surroundings. Congratulations, but your true transformational self begins to die. You are not able to be real, honest, and transparent because you are afraid of not fitting in any longer. You are actually being dwarfed and diminished in your spirit. If not allowed to come into an authentic encounter with God, your conformity mildly and gradually gives birth to full-blown hypocrisy. You are now in the form of something, but not truly representing your inner self, and your spirit has no power.

At one point, Paul's authority was in question at the Corinthian church.

> Now some are puffed up, as though I were not coming to you. But I will come to you shortly, if the Lord wills, and I will know, not the word of those who are puffed up, but the power. For the kingdom of God is not in <u>word but in power.</u>
>
> —1 Corinthians 4:18–20[*]

---

[*] Emphasis added

Form Follows Function!

When you are functioning in an authentic, transformational worship, looking in that glorious mirror, you will take on that divine image of the glory of God. Transformation comes from the root word *metamorphous.* It is what happens to a caterpillar when it becomes a butterfly or a tadpole when it becomes a frog. This brings up another aspect of transformation: You don't backslide from transformation; you can only backslide from conformity. You do not see the frog or butterfly going back to their former self . . . you did not just change, you grew. In transformation, you grow, you mature, you overcome. Conformity tries to put pressure on you to be like others think you should be. It actually applies additional pressure to what should be organic, spiritual development. Pulling on a blade of grass does not help it grow. But if it is watered and allowed sun and dirt to interact, given time, the grass will grow. Conformity can happen fast; transformation is slow, so that patience can have its perfect work.

> But let patience have its perfect work, that you may
> be perfect and complete, lacking nothing.
>
> —James 1:4

Another word for perfect and complete is mature, ripe, or fully developed.

Committed to the Process

Years ago, a group of us went to a local quarry swim hole. It was a great time filled with laughter, good friends, and good food. I went out to swim in a private section and noticed a high dive. When I say high dive, there was about a twelve-foot metal-framed diving board on the top of a quarried wall about sixteen feet straight up. As I was looking at this thing, I heard the Lord say to me, "I want you to climb up there and dive off; I want to teach you something." Now, that was funny. I'm not much of a diver, but I thought I'd give it a try. I climbed up the ladder on the side of the wall, then climbed up the other ladder of the metal-framed diving board. There was no one around, just me and the Lord. I looked down, and it got serious, I mean, it was high up there. I was thinking maybe I should just jump off, you know, or do a cannonball, but I heard again, "I want you to DIVE off so I can show you something." I did a couple quick calculations in my head as far as the distance I needed to dive out from the board. Then I put my fists together, extended my arms, and jumped headfirst off that board. As soon as my foot left the board, I heard the Lord say, **"Now you're committed."**

This was a revolutionary understanding of what it meant to be committed, and it changed my perspective completely. Up to that time, I believed being committed was holding on to something with all your might, holding on tooth and nail. It was completely dependent on my strength, my character, and my word, but this was completely different. I now understand that commitment is giving over, completely abandoning your-self and your strength and surrendering to the process. I could not get back up on that board no matter what I tried to do—I WAS COMMITTED, abandoned to the dive. I did land safely and swam back to join our friends, but I was different. Committing to transformational worship and being a living sacrifice is like diving off the board—and there is no going back.

CHAPTER 7: YOUR AUTHENTIC TESTIMONY

And they overcame him by the blood of the Lamb and by the word of their testimony, and they did not love their lives to the death.

—Revelation 12:11

People can challenge your doctrine; they can question your theology, but your authentic testimony has power. Please don't qualify your testimony as something that only happened a long time ago, something that is only limited to your initial salvation experience. If you are growing in faith, if you are walking with the living Christ, you're still writing your testimony. Your testimony is the living, authentic inner man growing as a believer, and it is part of you having authority—being authentic!

Now Abraham was old, well advanced in age; and the LORD had blessed Abraham in all things. So Abraham said to the oldest servant of his house, who ruled over all that he had, "Please, put your hand under my thigh, and I will make you swear by the LORD, the God of heaven and the God of the earth, that you will not take a wife for my son from the daughters of the Canaanites, among whom I dwell; but you shall go to my country and to my family, and take a wife for my son Isaac."

—*Genesis 24:1–4*

This exchange between Abraham and his servant was of the utmost importance to him. He made his servant swear by the Lord to be sure his son did not marry a Canaanite. Have you ever seen a movie or been in a courtroom where before someone stood on the witness stand, they would put their right hand on the Bible and swear to tell the truth, the whole truth, and nothing but the truth? Well, that's what's happening here between Abraham and his servant; it was a solemn oath. Only one difference—they didn't have a Bible. The Bible wasn't even written yet.

I saw a documentary once about ancient artwork. They were explaining and critiquing various aspects of art from different styles and time periods. The one I will always remember was an armored soldier standing before his king, and he was called to swear that he was telling the truth. Only he had both his hands crossed in front of him, the lower half. Then the narrator of the documentary shared how that in ancient times, they would swear by their lineage, by their future generations; they would swear by their children's, children's children. So testimony has to do with the male genital area. They would swear on their seed. In the above reference in Genesis 24, the second verse is a euphemism where it says, "Please, put your hand under my thigh." His servant was swearing on Abraham's lineage. You can't get more authentic than that. Your testimony has to do with who and what you really are and having enough intestinal fortitude to not just comply or conform under pressure, but to stand strong. Your fruitfulness and your future depend on it.

I heard someone say that "growing old is becoming the person you should have been your whole life." It's by your worship of the living and true God that you are being transformed into who God created you to be—and it's a lifelong transformation. My wife keeps threatening to write a book titled *The Man I'm Living with Is Not the Man I Married.* I'm hoping she means that in the most positive sense. ☺ I believe it's because of the transformation God has worked in me over the past forty-six years of marriage.

> *Then I heard a loud voice saying in heaven, "Now salvation, and strength, and the kingdom of our God, and the power of His Christ have come, for the accuser of our brethren, who accused them before our God day and night, has been cast down. And they*

> *overcame him by the blood of the Lamb and by the word of their testimony, and they did not love their lives to the death.*

> *—Revelation 12:10–12*

Your testimony is your real-life story and your actual encounter with the living God. It is where your authority flows from. It won't be something you repeat or echo from what someone else has said. Abraham's pledging his servant in a testimony was very important and had much to do with his future bloodline. Your testimony, in sync with the Holy Spirit working in you, will produce the word of God with reproductive power. Your authentic testimony is your life flow, and from that comes the power and authority behind the word you speak.

A SUMMARY

Then the eleven disciples went away into Galilee, to the mountain which Jesus had appointed for them. When they saw Him, they worshiped Him; but some doubted. And Jesus came and spoke to them, saying, "<u>All authority has been given to Me in heaven and on earth</u>. Go therefore and make disciples of all the nations, baptizing them in the name of the Father and of the Son and of the Holy Spirit, teaching them to observe all things that I have commanded you; and lo, I am with you always, even to the end of the age." Amen.

—Matthew 28:16–20[*]

After His death and resurrection, before His ascension, Jesus declared His victory over every principality and power, both in heaven and on earth. He establishes His sovereignty over all creation and commissions (co-mission) His disciples to make disciples in ALL the nations, baptize, and teach. Then He gives the reassurance that He will never leave or forsake

---

[*] Emphasis added

us and will always be with us, even to the end of the age. Paul, in his writing to the Ephesians, further unfurls this extension of commission to the Gentiles, saying:

> To me, who am less than the least of all the saints, this grace was given, that I should preach among the Gentiles the unsearchable riches of Christ, and to make all see what is the fellowship of the mystery, which from the beginning of the ages has been hidden in God who created all things through Jesus Christ; to the intent that now the _manifold wisdom of God might be made known by the church to the principalities and powers in the heavenly places_, according to the eternal purpose which He accomplished in Christ Jesus our Lord, _in whom we have boldness and access with confidence through faith in Him_. Therefore I ask that you do not lose heart at my tribulations for you, which is your glory. For this reason I _bow my knees_ to the Father of our Lord Jesus Christ, from whom the whole family in heaven and earth is named, that He would grant you, according to the riches of His glory, to be _strengthened with might through His Spirit in the inner man_, that Christ may dwell in your hearts through _faith_; that you, being _rooted and grounded in love_, may be able to comprehend with all the saints what is the width and length and depth and height—to _know the love of Christ which passes knowledge_; that you may be filled with all the fullness of God. Now to Him who is

*able to do exceedingly abundantly above all that we
ask or think, according to the <u>power that works in us,</u>
to Him <u>be glory in the church by Christ Jesus to all</u>
<u>generations, forever and ever.</u> Amen.*

—*Ephesians 3:8–21*[*]

There is so much more to cover concerning authority. In
Luke 9:1–2, Jesus gives His disciples authority to heal and cast
out demons, and Romans 13 deals with authority in govern-
ment. Spiritual warfare is another huge realm of authority.
Husband, wife, and family authority are in sequential submission to God-established authority. Agreement in prayer authority is another. As you can see, this realm of understanding
continues way beyond the intentions of this booklet. Please be
encouraged to pursue these once you understand and apply
what we've covered. The reason for not going further with this
subject is because of the "academic slippage" we are so prone
to adopt. I am praying for transformation, not information.
If we can comprehend the essence of authority from what we
have covered here and apply these principles, then the purpose of this book has been accomplished. The primary purpose
has been stated, but let me review some takeaways here.

1. Spiritual authority is centered and imparted by the
   Author of all creation.
2. Creativity and originality flow in concert with
   Authority.

---

[*] Emphasis added

3. We can submit to the Author willingly in worship.
4. Worship is a humble posture of submission and adoration.
5. Worship costs something.
6. We are always humble before our God.
7. Authority is transferred through worship and humble submission.
8. We are to walk under His authority.
9. You look like, act like, and become what you worship.
10. We should seek transformational growth, not the cloak of conformity.
11. Transformational growth partners with our authentic testimony.
12. Worshippers receive power and authority from Him alone.
13. Taking authority can be presumptuous by assuming what hasn't been given to us.

Finally, when Jesus conquered the devil through the cross and resurrection, we are assured that the prophecy spoken in Genesis was forever fulfilled.

> *And I will put enmity*
> *Between you and the woman,*
> *And between your seed and her Seed;*
> *He shall bruise your head,*
> *And you shall bruise His heel."*
>
> *—Genesis 3:15*

We, as worshipping members of His body, are promised to share in that victory. As Jesus bruised the serpent's head, and we are now members of His body, we shall also partner in this victorious act with Him and in Him.

> *Now I urge you, brethren, note those who cause divisions and offenses, contrary to the doctrine which you learned, and avoid them. For those who are such do not serve our Lord Jesus Christ, but their own belly, and by smooth words and flattering speech deceive the hearts of the simple. For your obedience has become known to all. Therefore, I am glad on your behalf; but I want you to be wise in what is good, and simple concerning evil. And the God of peace will crush Satan under your feet shortly. The grace of our Lord Jesus Christ be with you. Amen.*
>
> *—Romans 16:17–20*[*]

---

[*] Emphasis added

DEEP GLIMPSES SERIES

Having served in full-time ministry for over thirty-three years, I have delivered countless sermons and teachings. While many of these messages blur together, a select few stand out as profound revelations—insights that have left an indelible mark on my soul and fundamentally changed my life.

These messages emerged from personal transformative experiences and comprise the books featured here in the Deep Glimpses series.

Remembering Communion

Jesus instructed, "Do this in remembrance of me." As you approach communion, what do you remember? I identified a direct parallel between marriage and communion, noting that the elements we remember about marriage correspond directly to our relationship with Christ and one another. Furthermore, I believe that the Lord's Table should involve more interaction among believers, making the presented pattern inclusive and participative.

The Appliance Gifts

God bestows grace upon each of us, connecting us through gifts that serve the church by strengthening, encouraging, and serving one another. These gifts function much like household appliances, contributing to a healthy and whole spiritual habitation.

The Author of Authority

In addition to being a pastor, I also led worship, fostering a dynamic culture within our worship experiences. However, there came a time when I questioned the direction and purpose of our focus in worship. Worship is far more than mere performance; it is a venue for exchange, impartation, and endowment. Understanding this can profoundly enhance the power in our lives.

Being Effective Between a Rock and a Hard Place

I often felt overwhelmed with ministry tasks such as counseling, leadership meetings, and sermon preparation, while balancing my marriage and family. In desperation, I cried out to the Lord, "I feel like I'm between a rock and a hard place. His response was, "That's where you should be," and He showed me biblical positions to help equip me in making the most of those times.

Lord willing, there will be other books in this series, but for now my prayer is that you will be strengthened and encouraged with these insights and brought into a clearer understanding of your walk with the living God.

www.ingramcontent.com/pod-product-compliance
Lightning Source LLC
Chambersburg PA
CBHW071340130626
46556CB00004B/1964